25 Common Sales Objections & How To Overcome Them

A Quick-Study Reference Guide for the

- *Sales Manager*
- *Sales Trainer*
- *Experienced Salesperson*
- *Novice Salesperson*

Bob Taylor

Illustrations by Mark Braun

Published by
The Dartnell Corporation
4660 Ravenswood Avenue
Chicago, Illinois 60640
Boston • London • Sydney

© 1991 The Dartnell Corporation
Printed in the U.S.A. by Dartnell Press
ISBN 0-85013-192-8

Contents

CHAPTER 3

More Sales Tips and Reminders for Handling Objections   73

About the Author

Bob Taylor is president of Sales Counselors, a firm based in Glenview, Illinois, that provides training aids to large and small companies alike. He is the author of *Back to Basic Selling* (Prentice Hall), which was acclaimed by *The Wall Street Journal* as one of the best books on selling.

Bob has conducted seminars throughout the United States, Canada, and Latin America and has received numerous awards from the National Society of Sales Training Executives. He is a professional salesman with a record of continuous success in selling. As a professional, he enjoys developing others for the professions of salesmanship, sales training, and sales management.

Bob's company is a resource for hundreds of training aids and videos. The techniques he teaches are practical and realistic because they were learned from personal, front-line successful selling.

Synopsis

The best way to handle objections is to anticipate those objections that might arise and then prepare to handle them. Coping with objections is a normal part of the selling process. It is a "way of life" to the professional salesperson. The top performers recognize that fact and take objections into consideration as they plan each sales call.

Good salesmanship can prevent some objections from arising. The whole question of objections starts at the initiation of the sales contact. What you say and how you say it, what you do and how you do it, how you look and act — all have a tremendous influence in preventing and/or handling objections. This is why the first chapters of this book are of equal importance to those on the suggested treatment of the 25 most common sales objections.

Here is an overview of the many ideas offered in this book for planning and preparing for the handling of objections in each important sales interview (and telephone contact):

1. Learn as much as you can about the possible needs of the prospect.
2. Decide which item in your product line you will offer.
3. Decide which application of that product you will suggest.
4. Chart the benefits you think your prospect will enjoy by the use of the positive features of that product.
5. Program your brain with selling sentences that will concisely describe those benefits.

6. Gather and store in your briefcase the most appropriate testimonial letters from customers who have needs similar to the needs you suspect your prospect might have.

7. Prepare for the "stand-up" lobby interview. Have a separate folder of materials that can be quickly extracted from your briefcase and used as you stand in the lobby with your prospect. This special folder should contain the testimonials, charts, graphs, and other attention-getting materials that will aid you under adverse selling conditions.

8. Review and practice with appropriate success stories.

9. Review all the objections in this book with special attention to those you think might arise during the sales interview.

10. Consider how you might prevent some objections from arising by using certain statements, visuals, and techniques.

11. Practice your responses, including the techniques suggested in this book.

Accept the fact that encountering objections is a normal part of the selling process. Also accept the fact that many objections can be prevented. In addition, many objections that do arise can be successfully overcome by: 1) understanding their root causes and 2) using the right verbal responses synchronized with body language and the smooth use of sales tools. Words alone are not enough! And, last but not least, many objections, properly handled, can lead to the close.

But as in all parts of professional salesmanship, handling objections takes planning, preparing, executing, and evaluating. It doesn't just happen. Training for handling the objections problem must include all parts of a complete sales training program:

1. Product knowledge
2. Markets and application knowledge
3. Territory management
4. Time management
5. Sales techniques.

All five parts are interrelated in handling objections. For example:

1. Incomplete product knowledge can actually create objections.
2. Likewise, ignorance of the right markets and the correct applications can cause "self-inflicted" objections.
3. Bad territory management can prevent selective marketing which, in turn, can create unnecessary objections.
4. Good time management includes careful planning and preparation for each sales call. Such preparation anticipates objections and the effective responses to them.
5. Sales techniques include selling yourself as well as selling your product or service. Salespeople who employ the right techniques encounter fewer objections and make more sales.

This book is aimed at veteran as well as new sales representatives and sales managers.

Chapter 1 sets the stage for the following chapters by describing familiar sales situations and getting the reader to concentrate on the "objections problem."

Chapter 2 concentrates on dialogue and social interaction as vital parts of the selling process — and their importance in handling objections. This chapter also offers valuable ideas on benefit-feature selling and the development of selling sentences.

Chapter 3 describes personal impact and its importance to selling yourself. A positive personal impact can go a long way in preventing and handling objections. Conversely, a negative personal impact can create objections even though the product is right and the need is there. This chapter also "dissects" personal impact into four parts: body language, vocabulary, oral delivery, and dress and grooming. It also discusses the body language of both the seller and the buyer — and their great importance to the successful handling of objections.

Chapter 4 presents 13 common objections. Each one is handled in three parts:

1. Comments on the objection and possible causes of it
2. The suggested response, including body language and the use of sales tools
3. Your response (written in the reader's words).

Chapter 5 presents 12 additional common objections and, as in Chapter 4, offers for each, 1) comments, 2) suggested response, and 3) the reader's response. In addition, space is provided for additional objections that the reader and colleagues will want to use for objections that are peculiar to the industry.

Use this book to help you plan, prepare, execute, and evaluate each sales interview. Refer to it as you discuss the objection problem with your peers and sales manager. Put the ideas in this book together into "an ensemble of professionalism" that will reduce the number of objections you encounter and improve your "batting average" in overcoming those that do arise. The daily use of this book will increase your sales and earnings and will make selling fun as well as profitable.

Introduction

How often do you face the following sales objections and others like them?

- "Your price is too high."
- "I'm not interested."
- "I'll take it up with my management."
- "I'm satisfied with my present suppliers."
- "I'm too busy."
- "Drop something in the mail."
- "I'll think about it."

How well do you handle them? How many sales do you lose because of the objections problem?

Also, how successfully do you anticipate objections and plan your presentation to prevent objections from arising?

And do you use the objection as a sales opportunity?

If you are satisfied with your success in dealing with the objection problem, you don't need this book. However, if you do stumble over objections or if objections catch you by surprise, then this is the book for you.

Most training on handling sales objections is superficial. That is, the training is limited to the words to use in responding to the prospect's objections. That's why objections are such obstacles for many sales representatives — and why so many sales are lost. Effective training in handling objections should include an examination of the root causes of objections. Verbal responses should be synchronized with body language, the showing of testimonials, the telling of success stories, and the smooth handling of sales tools and visual aids.

The sales objection doesn't have to be a stumbling block. With the right perspective and preparation, many objections can be prevented and those that do arise can be successfully handled.

Handling objections is a normal part of selling. It is of equal importance in the traditional five steps to the sale:

1. Gaining favorable attention
2. Developing a dialogue
3. Making the proposal
4. Handling objections
5. Closing the sale.

As in the other four steps, successful handling of objections takes:

- Planning
- Preparation
- Execution.

The planning includes familiarity with all objections that are likely to arise.

The preparation includes practice with powerful responses to those objections including the use of visual aids and positive body language.

The execution is the culmination of the planning and practice in the form of verbal responses in combination with the use of visual aids, body language, testimonials, and success stories.

All types of selling — retail, service, and industrial — have certain common objections. For example, "Your price is too high" is a very common objection in all industries. Others are peculiar to the type of selling involved. For example, in retailing we are likely to encounter, "No thanks, I'm just looking."

Likewise, objections can arise in all forms of contact with prospects and customers such as:

- Face to face
- By telephone
- By mail

- By formal, written proposal.

Many objections are not really objections. They are just put-offs. When you get many put-offs or brush-offs, you had better review your sales presentation and your personal impact.

Also, many objections are sales opportunities. The successful handling of an objection can be the final step to the close and the order.

This book offers you many helpful objection-handling tips for many kinds of sales situations. It will get you thinking about how to successfully handle objections. So that's what this book is all about — how to handle objections and close more sales.

CHAPTER 1

Examples
Of Typical Sales Situations —
Including Sales Objections

This chapter presents some actual sales interviews that took place over a period of time. In all instances the names have been changed, but the principal facts remain. As a salesperson, you have probably observed and/or experienced hundreds of sales interviews like them. Likewise, as a potential buyer, you have probably offered many similar objections or put-offs in your business purchasing capacity and your personal shopping.

In many sales situations, the objections voiced are not the real reasons for the turndowns. When you can sense or discover the real reason for a turndown, you have a better chance of successfully handling the objection. Further, by employing appropriate tactics and behavior you can prevent some objections from arising.

The sales situations presented in this chapter have been designed to set the stage for the following chapters. The case studies will alert you to the possible root causes of the objection. In each case study, put yourself in the shoes of the prospect and measure the real needs against the actions and behaviors of the seller.

Be prepared to answer the questions at the end of each case study. These questions have been designed to help you put yourself in the shoes of the seller. Hint: One of the best ways to understand the actions of others is to study your own reactions to the unwanted telephone call or the poor sales presentation.

A Car Sale Situation

Mr. and Mrs. Robert Rogers are a middle-aged couple living in a suburb of a large city. Mr. Rogers is an executive and commutes to the city; therefore, Mrs. Rogers is the primary driver of the family car.

The car is five years old, and regular maintenance inspections have not been made on schedule. Mr. Rogers knows that is imprudent but his time is limited, and his car dealer service department is closed on weekends. Mrs. Rogers procrastinates on the car inspections because the dealer who sold them the car doesn't provide transportation while their car is being serviced. Further, up until very recently, the car has operated with few problems. However, several weeks ago the car stalled in heavy traffic — leaving Mrs. Rogers extremely frightened and frustrated. The problem was corrected, but now Mrs. Rogers is afraid that the stalling might happen again.

She is urging Mr. Rogers to trade in the car for a new one. He has agreed to do so.

Some of the Rogers's neighbors have reported some excellent "deals" in their car purchases. They boasted about the dollars off the sticker prices and the bargains won by extensive shopping. This has convinced the Rogerses that they too should enjoy financial savings in addition to the security of a brand new car. In addition, without really analyzing it or putting it into words, they would be much more comfortable if their new car was maintained by expert technical care. The stalling incident has bothered Mr. Rogers almost as much as it has troubled his wife.

So the Rogerses started out to "shop around" for a new car.

Ed Kennedy, a salesman for Jennings Buick, has been selling cars for seven years and is rated as one of the best in that Buick dealership. He was approached in the showroom by Mr. and Mrs. Rogers. After the usual polite greetings, Mr. Rogers opened up with this statement:

"Mrs. Rogers and I are shopping for a good price on a Buick four-door LeSabre. We are driving the same model now. It's five years old, and we'd like to trade it for the current model. We now have a charcoal gray and are looking for a blue or some other color. We want whitewall tires, a tilt wheel, and a tape deck. What do you have like that and what is the price?"

Ed invited Mr. and Mrs. Rogers into his office. After they were seated he said, "Let me have the keys to your car and I'll have our appraiser look it over. In the meantime, I'll tell you what we have in stock for immediate delivery."

Ed described the cars in stock that most nearly fit Mr. Rogers's specifications. While this was going on, the appraiser inspected the couple's car, returned with the keys, and placed a note on Ed's desk.

Ed showed the cars on display in the showroom and took his clients to the lot where certain cars were inspected in detail. He then brought Mr. and Mrs. Rogers back to his office and started to work on his calculator — as his prospects looked on in silence. Ed sensed they had been through this routine a number of times.

Finally, Ed completed his calculations and handed Mr. Rogers a paper containing his quotation. "Here's a good buy for you," Ed said. "We can have this car ready for you in two days. Shall I write it up?"

Mr. Rogers glanced at the figures and showed them to Mrs. Rogers. "Thank you Mr. Kennedy," Mr. Rogers said. "As I told you, we are shopping. Your price is too high. We will continue to look around. We may be back. Thank you for your time."

Phil Robertson, a salesman for the Loring Buick dealership, sold the Rogerses a new car. It fit the same specifications they described to Ed Kennedy of the Jennings Buick agency. The price was a bit higher than that quoted by Ed.

There was no calculator in sight as Phil engaged the Rogerses in a conversation. They discussed the Rogers's transportation needs and the good perfor- mance, up to the recent problem, of their five-year- old car. Phil soon learned that Mrs. Rogers was the primary driver — and of her new worries about stalling.

From that point on, Phil's sales presentation emphasized the quality of the new model LeSabre and the excellent reputation of the dealer service department. He demonstrated to the Rogerses how the agency's new computer system alerted customers to the need for checkups. He also outlined the transportation plan for service customers.

The main theme of Phil's sales talk was "worry free driving." The Rogerses were so impressed that the price factor became a secondary issue.

Questions and Exercises

1. What were the Rogerses really looking for in a new car?

   _____

   _____

   _____

   _____

   _____

   _____

2. What was the root cause of Mr. Rogers's objection to Ed Kennedy's proposal?

   _____

   _____

   _____

   _____

   _____

   _____

3. Write your comments about the presentations of Ed Kennedy of Jennings Buick and Phil Robertson of Loring Buick.

    _____

    _____

    _____

    _____

    _____

    _____

4. How can you use the ideas in this case study to improve your sales presentations and your "batting average" in handling objections?

    _____

    _____

    _____

    _____

    _____

    _____

A Furniture Sale Situation

Margaret Murray, a salesperson for the Plimpton Furniture Gallery, was called by the receptionist and informed that a customer needed some attention. Margaret went at once to the front of the store and met Mrs. Richard Allen. After the usual greetings, Mrs. Allen said that it was her first visit to the gallery and mentioned she had learned about it from a friend. She said, with a smile, that she needed some expert assistance. She had just redecorated her home and was now looking for a new couch for her living room. Fortunately she had brought samples of the carpeting and wallpaper. This, of course, was very helpful to Margaret in picturing the appropriate color for the couch.

Margaret conducted Mrs. Allen through the gallery and they inspected a number of choices. They finally came to a couch that had the right dimensions and style — and the color seemed to be ideal in

conjunction with the carpeting and wallpaper. After considerable discussion Mrs. Allen paused, slowly shook her head, and said:

"I'm sorry. I think the color is right and I like it, but I don't like the print."

Questions

1. Is this a legitimate objection or a put-off?

_____

_____

_____

_____

_____

_____

2. What should Margaret do now?

_____

_____

_____

_____

_____

_____

3. Is such resistance common in your business?

_____

_____

_____

_____

_____

_____

4. If so, what is the best way to handle it?

_____

_____

_____

_____

_____

_____

A Car Service Situation

Bob Burton has driven the same car for seven years. Routinely, in October of each year, he took it to his favorite car dealer for winterizing. This included an oil change, a check of the cooling system, and a general inspection to prepare for winter driving.

George Nelson, Bob's favorite service advisor in the service department, knew the car and was always especially attentive to Bob. This made Bob comfortable in his dealings with the car agency, and he usually acted on the service advice offered.

But on his latest visit, Bob learned that George Nelson was no longer with the dealership, and a new service advisor, Jim Dufca, was on duty. Bob explained the winterizing he wanted done, and the necessary papers were filled out. Bob left the car and walked back to his office.

In about two hours, Bob received a telephone call from Jim, who said, "Mr. Burton, we have your car on the rack and the technician and I have looked it over. First, we checked the cooling system and it's okay. We also changed your oil. But we found some things that should be corrected. Your front linkage is worn, and the center link should be replaced. I also recommend that you let us repack the wheel bearings, rotate the tires, balance the wheels, and align the front end."

Bob Burton immediately asked about the additional costs and was told that the repair bill would be at least four times the usual cost for the routine winterizing. He told Jim, "I can't afford that at this time. Let's just stick to the service I ordered. The car is seven years old. Perhaps I'll trade it in next year. Thanks for your call."

Questions

1. Was working with the new service advisor a possible cause for Bob's objection to the extra work and costs? Write your thoughts on this.

   _____

   _____

   _____

   _____

   _____

   _____

2. What losses to Bob could occur if the additional work is not done right now?

   _____

   _____

   _____

   _____

   _____

   _____

3. How could Jim Dufca respond and overcome Bob's objection? Write a convincing response.

   _____

   _____

   _____

   _____

   _____

   _____

A Service Contract Sale Situation

Rich Harold is a service engineer for the Pritchard Instrument Company. He has managed the same service territory for five years and has won an excellent reputation with his customers. The regular preventive maintenance calls on his service contract users have been particularly helpful in developing rapport and a trusting relationship with the operators as well as management. And, of course, emergency repair service has given Rich the opportunity to demonstrate his technical expertise — as well as his deep concern for his customers. Because of his good work, he enjoys a high rate of service contract renewals.

However, Rich does have a problem with one customer concerning the contract. It is the Research Laboratory of the State University. Dr. Millard Morris, the lab director, is resisting Rich's attempts to renew the service contract. During Rich's last preventive maintenance call, Dr. Morris said, "We have had no trouble with the equipment for the past two years.

The only service I have seen is your regular inspection service. My budget is tight and your contract
price is high. Under the circumstances, to continue
that expense is unjustified."

Questions

1. How should Rich respond to Dr. Morris's objec-
    tion? Write a response.

    _____

    _____

    _____

    _____

    _____

    _____

2. During the course of the present preventive
    maintenance contract, what could Rich have
    done to prevent the objection from arising?

    _____

    _____

    _____

    _____

    _____

    _____

A Woman's Clothing Sale Situation

Joanne Hastings was an experienced salesperson for an exclusive store specializing in ladies' dresses and suits. She maintained a file on each of her regular customers and was on the alert for new garments that would fit the tastes of those clients.

There was a disturbing slowdown of business in the store, and Joanne tried desperately to do something about it. When a fresh shipment of dresses came in from New York, she immediately called many of her good customers. One call was to Mrs. Susan Ellis, who agreed to come in to see some of the garments Joanne had described on the telephone.

Mrs. Ellis tried on several dresses as requested and was lukewarm about them. Finally Joanne brought out one that was gray with short sleeves.

Mrs. Ellis immediately shook her head and,

looking disapprovingly at Joanne, said, "Joanne, gray is not my color. It's too dull. And you *know* that with my heavy arms I can't wear short sleeves."

Joanne created that objection. She had her file on previous purchases and comments by Mrs. Ellis, so she knew her favorite colors and other problems such as short sleeves. The slowdown of business had made Joanne overeager for the sale, so she committed the error of putting her needs before those of her loyal customers. It took quite a while before she regained the confidence of Mrs. Ellis.

Questions

1. How can you use your knowledge of the needs and "hot buttons" of your customers and prospects?

_____

_____

_____

_____

_____

_____

2. How can you avoid the same error committed by Joanne?

_____

_____

_____

_____

_____

_____

A Business Form Sale Situation

Marion Martin is a star salesperson for the Morrison Business Forms and Systems Corporation. Her organization specializes in designing and printing forms for various business systems such as order/invoice; payroll; production control; and purchase/receiving operations. Marion is an expert in surveying the present operations of the prospect, determining the needs for improvement, designing the forms for the new system, and closing the sale. It is one of the highest forms of salesmanship, and Marion is good at it.

Marion is now working with a new client, the Reliance Manufacturing Corporation. She has completed a survey of the prospect's operations and has designed the forms for her proposed improvements of Reliance's invoicing and accounts receivable procedures. She is explaining her plans to Mr. Russell Hanson, the comptroller at Reliance. Mr. Hanson is enthusiastic and has commented favorably on the clever design of the forms. He also seems to grasp the many benefits of the new system — and he doesn't indicate any negative reaction to the price of the installation. But when Marion asks for the final decision, Mr. Hanson shakes his head and says, "Don't go so fast, Ms. Martin. I'll have to go over this more carefully and then take it up with our management group. Leave this material with me, and I'll get back to you. Thank you for all your good ideas."

Questions

1. What should Marion do now?

_____

_____

_____

_____

_____

_____

2. Do you experience similar resistances? How do
    you handle them?

_____

_____

_____

_____

_____

_____

A Retail Sale Situation

It was a busy day in the Marshall Department
Store. There were many customers browsing around,
and the clerks were actively ringing up sales. Finally,
during a lull, Mary Martin, a salesperson, spotted a
stylishly dressed lady inspecting some expensive
dresses. She was looking intently at one in particular.
Mary approached the lady and asked, "May I help
you?"

The lady turned, smiled at Mary and started to
walk away as she replied, "No. I'm just looking."

Questions and Exercises

1. Is this a common occurrence in retail selling? Explain why this might be so.

   _____

   _____

   _____

   _____

   _____

   _____

2. Write your comments about the possible responses Mary Martin can use in this sales situation.

   _____

   _____

   _____

   _____

   _____

   _____

A Cosmetic Sale Situation

After Mr. and Mrs. Ralph Burgess completed their annual task of selecting Christmas cards in their favorite store, Agnes said to Ralph, "I'm going over to see Eileen in Cosmetics to get some moisturizer and lipstick. I'll meet you at the car."

Mrs. Burgess liked to work with Eileen, a very efficient sales lady in the Cosmetic Department. Eileen kept an accurate file on the likes and dislikes of her customers. She has been dealing with Agnes Burgess for many years and a comfortable buyer/ seller relationship has been developed.

But Eileen was not at work that day so a new salesperson, Helen Dugan, waited on Mrs. Burgess. Fortunately, Mrs. Burgess remembered the brand names and details of her previous purchases so there was no problem for Helen in handling the sale. When the transaction was completed Helen said, "Mrs. Burgess, while you are here I'd like to have you sample a brand new fragrance. It's a perfume we have just received from France. May I put some on your wrist?" Mrs. Burgess sampled the perfume and said it was excellent.

But when Helen showed the beautifully designed bottle and quoted the price, Mrs. Burgess shook her head and said, "Oh, no. That's way over my budget. I wouldn't dare go to that expense. Thank you very much. Goodbye."

Questions

1. Do you think this was an objection or a put-off?

   _____

   _____

   _____

   _____

   _____

   _____

2. Eileen has had many years of experience in selling to Agnes Burgess. How do you think she would have handled this perfume sale?

   _____

   _____

   _____

   _____

   _____

   _____

An Office Equipment Sale Situation

Bill Pritchard is a salesman for the Monarch Office Equipment Company. His company distributes an excellent line of equipment including copiers. Commissions for copier sales are high, so Bill has been spending most of his selling time on them.

Most of Bill's work has been "cold calls" on prospects and customers. He found that he can get around pretty fast that way. But his call reports show a lot of calls and very few sales. His sales manager called Bill in to his office for a conference. Bill's boss pointed out the low ratio of sales to the high number of calls. The record also showed a high number of "lobby interviews" and quick put-offs. The sales manager suggested a better mix of appointment calls to cold calls. Bill agreed and started a program of calling prospects for appointments.

Bill knows that architects are good prospects for copiers because they must duplicate their specifications. He selected some names from the Yellow Pages and started his telephoning.

One "suspect" that he thought might be a prospect was Burke, Boswell and Boyle Company, a large and well-known firm of architects. Bill called the company and asked for the name of the office manager. He was given Ralph Cooper's name. He asked to speak to Mr. Cooper and when Mr. Cooper came on the line Bill said, "Mr. Cooper, this is Bill Pritchard of the Monarch Office Equipment Company. How are you today?"

"I'm fine but very busy," Mr. Cooper said. "What can I do for you?"

Bill said, "I'd like to come in to see you about my line of copiers. They are the best copiers on the market today. I'd like to give you a demonstration at your convenience. Would 10 o'clock tomorrow morning be okay or would the afternoon be better?"

Mr. Cooper replied, "I appreciate your call, but I'll be in meetings all day tomorrow. Why don't you drop something in the mail."

Questions

1.   Write your analysis of this sales situation and the root cause of the objection.

   _____

   _____

   _____

   _____

   _____

   _____

2.   How do you respond to the "Drop something in the mail" objection?

   _____

   _____

   _____

   _____

   _____

   _____

An Industrial Sale Situation

Bill Stevens's sales production was only fair and he was getting worried. He is a sales representative for the Ace Fastener Company. Bill has increased his number of calls but so far that has done nothing to solve his problem. The situation is particularly frustrating because of the number of objections and put-offs he is getting.

It was raining as Bill drove into a prospect's parking lot. It had rained all morning, and Bill's raincoat was soaked. He grabbed his briefcase and dashed for the lobby entrance.

The receptionist told Bill that the purchasing agent was Ralph Morgan, and she called Mr. Morgan's secretary.

Ralph Morgan was working under pressure. His boss had asked for a report by 3 p.m. When Miss Agnew, his secretary, told him of Bill Stevens's presence in the lobby, he was at first inclined to deny him an interview. But his company had told him that he should treat visiting salespeople as he expected the company's own sales representatives to be treated. So Ralph reluctantly left his desk and went to the lobby. He discovered long ago that the lobby interview was an easy way to get rid of unwanted salespeople.

In the meantime, Bill sat down in the lobby, opened his raincoat, lit a cigarette, and chose a magazine from a nearby table. His briefcase was unopened and rested on the floor beside him.

Ralph Morgan entered the lobby, and the receptionist handed him Bill's card and nodded in his direction. Bill stood up as Ralph Morgan approached him.

Ralph Morgan smiled as he extended his hand. "Good morning, Mr. Stevens. I'm Ralph Morgan. What can I do for you?" He remained standing so Bill was compelled to do likewise.

Bill smiled as he shook hands and said, "Good morning, Mr. Morgan. I'm with the Ace Fastener Corporation, and I've got a new design I'd like to show you."

He picked up his briefcase and looked around for a place to set it to open it up. He finally pulled out a sample and handed it to his prospect. "Here it is, Mr. Morgan," Bill said. "I brought this along as a sample of the kind of work we do. We can design fasteners for your specific needs."

Mr. Morgan looked at the sample and handed it back as he said, "Thank you, Mr. Stevens. We don't need anything like that. I appreciate your interest in us, but we are well satisfied with our present suppliers. Thanks for coming in."

Questions and Exercises

1. Ralph Morgan, like all buyers, wants to feel secure in his dealings with sellers. His buying reputation, as well as his company's welfare, depends on his selection of selling companies represented by professional salespeople. Write your comments concerning Bill's appearance and behavior.

_____

_____

_____

_____

_____

_____

2. How do you avoid such a put-off?

    _____

    _____

    _____

    _____

    _____

    _____

3. How do you prepare for a lobby interview?

    _____

    _____

    _____

    _____

    _____

    _____

4. Do you study the impact you make on customers and prospects?

_____

_____

_____

_____

_____

_____

5. What influence does your personal impact have on the *prevention* of put-offs and objections?

_____

_____

_____

_____

_____

_____

A Video Sale Situation

Rita Reilly is a telemarketing sales representative for Training Media, Inc., a producer and distributor of video training materials. Her company sells and rents films and videos to reinforce the clients' training programs.

Rita's job is to call suspects, prospects, and customers to acquaint them with videos that might be of specific aid in their training efforts. Rita has learned to cope with many objections to her proposal, but some are most difficult to handle. Her call to the Anderson Manufacturing Company is an example.

Rita has just learned about Anderson Manufacturing. She was told that Neil Perkins, the training director, has embarked on an extensive program that might require videos to augment classroom instruction. After several attempts, Rita was finally able to reach Mr. Perkins by telephone.

At first Neil Perkins was very courteous and attentive in the opening discussion, but then he interrupted Rita by asking, "Did you say you represent Training Media, Inc.? I'm sorry, I didn't catch that name at first. Miss Reilly, I have had a bad experience with your company, and I don't want to do business with you again."

Questions

1. If you were Rita Reilly, how would you respond to Neil Perkins?

    _____

    _____

    _____

    _____

    _____

    _____

Summary

This chapter examines many common sales situations that we see every day in our personal and business selling and buying experiences and was designed to set the stage for the chapters that follow.

We'll find out that some objections are real and can't be overcome. Other objections are raised because of conscious or subconscious resistance to the product or proposition — or even the seller.

As stated in the Introduction, handling objections is a way of life in selling. It is important that you accept that fact. Handling objections is of equal importance in the five steps to the sale:

1. Gaining favorable attention
2. Developing a dialogue
3. Making the proposal
4. Handling objections
5. Closing the sale.

The case studies and questions in this chapter were designed to help you concentrate on the objection-handling step to the sale. It is important, however, to remember that the professional execution of the other four steps has an important influence on your success with the objections problem.

After reading this book it is suggested that you review this chapter and your answers to the questions that follow the case studies.

CHAPTER 2

Sales Tips and Reminders for Handling Objections

Handling Objections Requires Complete Sales Training

Mastering the objections problem requires a solid foundation of:
1. Product knowledge
2. Knowledge of the various markets — and the applications of the products to each market
3. Selling skills and basic psychology
4. The right attitude, which is based on the firm belief that the purchase of the product will offer measurable benefits to the buyer.

The Five Major Parts Of the Average Sales Interview

As previously emphasized, there are five important steps to the sale. For example, in the sales contact (either face to face or by telephone), the interview can be roughly divided into these parts:
1. Gaining favorable attention
2. Developing a dialogue

3. Making the proposal
4. Handling objections
5. Closing the sale.

The sequence can vary with each contact. In fact, the need for handling objections can arise very early in the interview. The point is that handling objections is a major step to the sale — and must be included in the planning of the sales interview.

The Importance of Dialogue And Social Interaction

Some products are so unique and the need for them so vital that they seem to "sell themselves." Conversely, other products are very similar — if not identical — to those of many competitors. These products and services require the skills of professional salespeople. In other words, *the salespeople make the difference.* It is *salesmanship* that provides the winning edge.

Salesmanship is the art of determining the prospect's needs, making sure the product will fill those needs, proving it, and completing a transaction that is mutually beneficial to both the buyer and the seller. To accomplish this, the buyer must be sold

both on the product *and on the seller of that product.*
If the seller is pleasing as well as assuring to the
buyer, the buyer will respond by wanting to do
business with that particular salesperson. That is
why dialogue and social interaction are so important
to the sales representative.

Social interaction (which, of course, includes
dialogue) is the process by which people influence
other people through the mutual interchange of
thoughts, feelings, and reactions. We see it every day
in our business and social lives.

A satisfying social interaction between the
seller and the prospective buyer is best described by
the words "assuring" and "pleasing." The buyer must
be assured that the deal with the seller is good for the
buying person as well as the buying company.

One of the greatest fears that a buyer has is that
a bad purchase (perhaps involving quality or deliv-

ery) could bring personal criticism on the buyer or create loss of time, money, and delays for the company. This fear is the basis for many objections.

In addition to being assured, the buyer will be much more inclined to place an order with a salesperson who pleases than one who doesn't.

Techniques for Pleasing and Persuading

The techniques for pleasing and persuading used in social interaction are built on the urges, emotions, and needs of human nature:

- The need to be needed
- The need to be wanted
- The need to contribute something
- The need to be important to other people.

When one person fills a basic need of another, the receiver gains a thing of value and is instinctively impelled to give something of value in return to the one who has filled that need. Translating that into selling language, if the buyer receives something that is really needed and wanted from you, the buyer is instinctively motivated to give you what is perceived you want and need.

A Definition of Value

In psychological language, the word *value* covers areas far beyond the normal interpretation of the word. Value can be dollar value, such as cost savings to the buyer or an order for you. Value to the prospect can also include many other things, such as:

- Favorable reaction to your appearance
- Pleasant relationship with you, the seller
- Ease of understanding
- Appeal to pride
- Feeling of importance
- Favorable reaction to your obvious respect for the buyer and the buyer's time
- Enjoyment of the dialogue
- A comfortable feeling that you are "in sync" with the buyer
- A feeling of trust in dealing with you.

The Exchange of Values

When you and your prospect are face to face (or in contact by telephone), something more than communication is going on: not only information but also *value* is being exchanged. For example, when your prospect receives something of value from you — even something small like a smile, good eye contact, a nod of the head, or a complimentary remark — the prospect is impelled to reciprocate by giving you something of value, such as:

- More information concerning his or her problems
- Willingness to spend more time in the discussion
- Agreement to a survey of the present methods
- Agreement to buy your product or service.

Similarly, body language, the use of visual aids, the use of success stories and testimonials, and the smooth handling of sales tools are all of psychological value. They not only assure understanding, but they also please because of the professional way they are handled.

Involve your prospect in dialogue. Ask questions, indicate sincere interest in the buyer as a person, solicit opinions, make rewarding or complimentary remarks, listen intently (with your eyes as well as your ears), signify agreement, and use the paraphrase. Do what comes naturally based on plain social perception.

A good way to check this out is to study your own reactions to people. Ask yourself: "How do I react to a good listener, a friendly smile, the concise, pictorial explanation of a proposal, and suggestions worded in terms of benefits to me?"

Your self-examination will make it easier to understand the human factors of persuasion used every day by thousands of successful people. They are successful in human relations — and in selling. In fact, selling *is* human relations.

People buy with their hearts as well as with their heads. Little, seemingly insignificant, things influence them for or against the product, the seller, and the seller's company. Don't ever forget that. Your planned sales presentation and your handling of objections must include selling yourself as well as selling your product or service.

What Top Performers Have in Common

Psychologists have recently studied the common characteristics of the top performers in hundreds of sales forces. They discovered that most of the star salespeople excel in social interaction — the ability to engage a prospect in dialogue. They do this through probing and asking test questions early in the interview to search out the prospect's needs, to check for understanding of the proposition, and to test the mood of the buyer.

This social interaction helps to gain the favorable attention that is so vital in the initial stages of the contact with the prospect and customer. After you have developed a good presence and pleased the prospect, the stage is set for determining the needs and then proposing methods for serving those needs. *The development of social interaction will go a long way toward preventing objections from arising.*

Further, for those objections that can't be prevented, the response must be designed to keep the dialogue going so as to uncover the real reasons for the objection — and to keep the door open for the completion of the sale.

This is why the following tips and suggested responses to the objections will emphasize body language, visual aids, testimonials, success stories, sales tools, and other sales techniques in addition to the verbal responses. These suggested combinations help prevent the prospect from closing the interview and help you to continue the dialogue and proceed to the close.

Nine Questions In the Mind of the Buyer

In preparing for the telephone call and sales interview, keep in mind the following nine questions that are in the mind of the prospect. (Note: The buyer may not be conscious of these questions, but they are there just the same.) Plan your sales presentation to answer these questions:

1. Why should I see you?
2. Why should I listen?
3. What's my problem?
4. How is it solved?
5. Why should I trust you?
6. Why should I trust your company?
7. Why is your solution best?
8. Why should I take action?
9. Why should I take action *now*?

The 13 Possible Causes of Objections

In very general terms, objections can be caused by:

1. Time and work pressures
2. Complacency
3. Price above the ability to pay
4. Price not measured against value
5. A bad experience with the method, product, or company
6. Lack of information
7. Misinformation
8. Misunderstanding
9. Fear of criticism
10. Lack of rapport
11. Lack of a trusting relationship
12. An honest no-need for the product or the product doesn't meet the specifications
13. Poor selection of prospects.

Methods for Handling or Preventing Objections

Objections can be handled or prevented by:
1. Clarity in the sales presentation
2. Value weighed against price
3. Proofs by testimonials, success stories, and demonstrations
4. Effective communication
5. Empathy with the prospect and the understanding of the stress caused by time and work pressures
6. Rapport and a trusting relationship with the prospect
7. Clear statements of benefits produced by the positive features
8. Pacing and "mirroring" the prospect's mood and manner, body language, speech, and delivery
9. Practiced sales presentations and the smooth handling of sales tools
10. Personal impact, and professional conduct and appearance
11. Selective prospecting.

Selective Prospecting

Whenever possible, select your prospects from business classifications in which the need for your product is known. You can do this by checking your company's *customer* records. Learn as much as you can about the successful applications of your products by satisfied customers. Why did they buy? What

was the need for your product? What measurable
benefit does your customer enjoy by the application
of your product? The chances are very good that the
prospects in the same business classification will
have those same needs. This knowledge guides you
in your preparation for the contact with the prospect.
It will suggest:

1. Opening sentences designed to create
   favorable attention
2. Testimonial letters that will be of greatest
   interest to your prospect
3. Success stories relating to the solving of
   problems for a customer who had the same
   needs
4. Probing questions that are pertinent to the
   prospect's possible needs.

How to Use the S.I.C. Index

The S.I.C. (Standard Industrial Classification)
Index is ideal for selective prospecting. It is produced by the federal government and can be found in
all manufacturers and service directories. Almost any
library has copies in its business section. Many state
directories can be purchased from Manufacturers'
News, Inc., 4 East Huron Street, Chicago, IL 60611,
(312) 337-1084.

Here is an example of using the S.I.C. Index for
selecting your most likely prospects. Suppose one of
your company's best customers is an envelope
manufacturer. You call on that customer and find out
how your product is used and the benefits the
customer enjoys by that use. In the alphabetical
section of the State Directory you will find your
customer's name and the S.I.C. number. The number
for envelope manufacturers is 2677. You then turn to

the numerical index in the same directory, and, under the number 2677, you will find all the envelope manufacturers in the state. You will have the name of each company and the town it is located in.

The next step is to turn to the town index, where you will find the name of the non-user envelope company (your prospect), plus very important information such as: the street address, telephone

number, FAX number, the names of the company officers, the number of employees, and the number of square feet occupied.

When you call the number of the prospect, you ask to speak to the person who has the same *function* as that of your envelope *customer.* Your opening remarks are in the vocabulary of the envelope industry and, of course, you will be prepared to use success stories that describe the benefits of your product in that industry. And the chances are very good that your prospect in that industry has the same needs as your customers.

When you use such selective prospecting measures, you gain and hold the prospect's favorable attention, thus reducing the possibility of an objection or put-off. (And when you can describe your customer's successful operations, your enthusiasm shows through and becomes contagious.)

Success Stories

Your study of successful installations and satisfied customers will also provide you with a treasure house of stories you can relate at the proper time to cautious prospects. Build each success story on a framework of:

- Who was it?
- What was the problem?
- How did you solve it?
- Where did this happen?
- When did it occur?
- Why did the customer buy?
- What were the results (benefits)?

In planning your call, select the most appropriate stories and rehearse the telling of them.

Success stories are especially helpful when responding to an objection. For example: "I can understand how you feel (prospect). Mr. _____ of the (company name) felt the same way, but that company is now one of my best customers. Here's what happened." Then tell the success story.

Testimonials

Testimonials are written proofs of customer satisfaction. Like success stories, they are used to assure the prospect that you know what you are doing and that others have found you good to do business with.

Testimonial letters are easy to obtain. When a customer indicates satisfaction with your product or service, you simply ask, "Could you please give me a letter on that so I can show it to my prospects?" Develop a library of such testimonials and select appropriate ones for each specific call.

Another version of the testimonial letter is a "composite" of customer letterheads. Buy some black 8-1/2" x 11" paper and plastic transparent covers. Clip the tops of customer letterheads and paste them to the black paper. When you do this on both front and back of one black sheet, you will have accumulated approximately 20 letterhead tops. Have this

visual aid ready to use. In a quick glance, the prospect can see the names of about 20 satisfied customers. He or she may be familiar with some of those names. This is a powerful sales tool to use in answer to an objection and as part of your assurance techniques.

Use of the Prospect's Name

Call the buyer by name and use it frequently. Take care to learn the name before the call. Make sure you have it right. The frequent use of the prospect's name tends to hold the buyer's attention. You can also use it to indicate a change of pace. For example, after a successful response to an objection, you can say: "Now, (prospect's name), when may I deliver this?"

It's also smart to learn and use the names of all those you encounter along the way. Make notes of them and use them on your return visits. For example, place the name of the secretary in parenthesis next to the prospect's name — and use it when you call again.

Be careful about using first names too soon. Let the prospect set the pace.

Use of the Probing Question

The probing question is an important "trigger" to the dialogue. When given in the form of an open-ended question, it is almost certain to elicit a response from the buyer. An open-ended question is one that can't be answered with a mere "yes" or "no." Use questions that start with: "what," "where," "why," "who," "how," and "when." Here are some examples:

"(Prospect's name), *what* are your most critical requirements in the _____ area?"

"(Prospect's name), *where* do you plan to do this?"

"*Why* are you doing it this way?"

"*How* do you plan to ship this?"

"*When* are you scheduled to build it?"

The probing question, followed by a pause or

long silence, will usually prompt the prospect to respond and divulge the information you are seeking. Then additional probing questions will keep the information flowing. The probing question is almost always used in combination with positive body language and rewarding remarks.

Use of the Test Question

The test question is a means of getting agreement point by point and being on the alert for disagreement or disbelief. It helps the prospect make the closing decision by making minor decisions along the way. Here are some examples:

"That's what you want, isn't it, Bill?"

"We can agree on that, can't we?"

"How does that look to you, Mrs. _____?"

As you plan for the sales call, program your brain with test questions and use them during your sales interview. Their effective use will reduce the number of objections.

Features, Benefits, and Selling Sentences

A positive feature of a product (or service) is something of special value to the

prospect — something that can be used to fill the need of the prospect. It can be a physical feature of a device or it can be a key point in a proposition. Here are some examples of positive features:

- Good quality
- Accuracy
- Speed
- Strength
- Reasonable price
- Capacity
- Prompt shipment.

A benefit is something of value provided by the positive feature. Benefits are the things that result by the prospect's use of the positive feature. Here are some examples of benefits:

- Protection against downtime
- Savings of money
- Increase in profits
- Longer wear
- Reduction of costs
- Repeat business
- Increase in sales
- Peace of mind
- Praise from the boss
- Protection against injury
- More customer satisfaction.

Charting the features and benefits in your preparation for the sales call is an excellent way to "psyche yourself up" for the call. It clarifies your thinking and helps you program your brain with powerful selling sentences. Thus, by taking the offensive instead of the defensive, you prevent some objections from arising and you prepare to respond to those that do arise. The charting can be a very simple procedure on a single sheet of paper — like this:

Benefits

1. More profits
2. Attract more customers and sell more items.

Positive Features

1. Glass door in the merchandiser makes the product visible.
2. Positioned near the door creates impulse buying.

A *selling sentence* is the statement you make during the sales presentation to describe the *benefit* the prospect will enjoy as the result of using the *positive feature*. Because the benefit is of greater concern to the prospect, you open the sentence by stating the benefit and then quickly follow it up with mention of the positive feature. Here's an example:

"(Name of prospect), you will make *more profits [benefit]* and *attract more customers [benefit]* by allowing us to install this beautiful *glass door merchandiser*" *[positive feature]*.

The Rewarding Remark

This is an everyday bit of social interaction that is used in the business as well as the social world. It plays an important part in the dialogue. In the buyer-seller relationship, the *rewarding remark* used by the salesperson will encourage the prospect to continue the conversation and provide even more details of the operation — and problems. Use remarks such as:

"That's interesting."

"Tell me more!"

"Good thinking!"

"I understand how that could happen."

"That's excellent!"

"That was good timing."

The rewarding remark is accompanied by positive body language such as the smile, head nod, head shake, and leaning forward to indicate intense interest.

The Paraphrase

The paraphrase is a repetition of a person's recent statement in your own interpretation of those words. When you say:

"A moment ago you said, '_____ _____ _____,'" you reinforce the prospect's words. You also show that you are carefully listening and have respect for the prospect and the ideas advanced.

The *paraphrase* is an excellent tactic for continuing the dialogue and building rapport — and another means of preventing objections and put-offs.

The Appeal to Pride

An *appeal to pride* is a sincere compliment for something the buyer or the buyer's company has done — or it could be a favorable remark concerning the personnel in the buyer's office, the office decor, the friendly manner of the receptionist, or any other aspect of the operation.

Summary

This chapter emphasizes that handling objections is a major step in the traditional five steps to the sale. Each step depends on the successful completion of the other four. All five steps take training, planning, and preparation — as well as their professional execution.

This chapter also emphasizes the importance of building rapport and a trusting relationship between the buyer and the seller. The buyer must be sold on the product or service and on the seller of that product or service. This requires expert social interaction which is described in this and the following chapter.

The benefit-feature portion of this chapter is of extreme importance to the successful handling of objections. It forces the salesperson to think very objectively about the proposition and the honest advantages to the buyer. When the *right* product is presented to fit the *real* needs of the buyer, the transaction becomes a good purchase as well as a good sale. This win/win sales situation creates a sincere and enthusiastic attitude which, in turn, prevents some objections from arising.

Once again, the successful handling of objections is more than the mere mouthing of words in responding to the prospect's resistances. It takes complete knowledge of your product and markets, selective prospecting, social interaction, insight into your prospect's reactions, use of success stories and testimonials, benefit-feature charting, selling sentences, and the right attitude.

It is suggested that you review this chapter and then answer the following questions.

Review Questions and Exercises

1. Write your comments on the importance of
    product knowledge, markets and applications
    knowledge and an enthusiastic attitude in the
    handling of objections.

    _____

    _____

    _____

    _____

    _____

    _____

2. Why is it important to please and assure the
    buyer as well as sell the benefits and features of
    your product or service?

    _____

    _____

    _____

    _____

    _____

    _____

3. Write your definition of *salesmanship.*

_____

_____

_____

_____

_____

_____

4. Write your description of *social interaction.*

_____

_____

_____

_____

_____

_____

5. Why is social interaction important in selling —
    and in handling objections?

    _____

    _____

    _____

    _____

    _____

    _____

6. Review a recent sales objection you encoun-
    tered. Write your analysis of the possible cause
    of that objection. (Use the list of "Possible
    Causes of Objections," as shown in this chapter.)

    _____

    _____

    _____

    _____

    _____

    _____

7. Select the name of one of your company's best customers. Determine the S.I.C. number of that customer. Then list five names of suspects with the same S.I.C. number.

_____

_____

_____

_____

_____

_____

8. Why does selective prospecting reduce the number of objections and put-offs?

_____

_____

_____

_____

_____

_____

9.   Select a good customer and develop a success story about the benefits that customer is enjoying by the use of your company's products.

_____

_____

_____

_____

_____

_____

10.   Within the next 30 days, get from at least five satisfied customers testimonial letters concerning their use of your company's products.

_____

_____

_____

_____

_____

_____

11. Select a prospect and chart the benefits and
     features of your proposition.

     _____

     _____

     _____

     _____

     _____

     _____

12. From the charting exercise in question number
     11, write a powerful selling sentence.

     _____

     _____

     _____

     _____

     _____

     _____

CHAPTER 3

More Sales Tips and Reminders for Handling Objections

This chapter contains more on the importance of social interaction in handling objections. It emphasizes the need for the development of a positive *personal impact.* A favorable impression (impact) is vital to your success in developing rapport and a trusting relationship with your prospect. And when you accomplish *that,* you have solved many of your objection problems.

Personal Impact — What It Is and What It Does

Personal impact is the total impression you make on others through your:
- Body language (gestures, postures, and eye contact)
- Vocabulary
- Oral delivery
- Dress
- Grooming.

Your personal impact can be either positive or negative. The positive personal impact you wish to develop and employ must be based on what the buyer wants and needs. The average buyer wants assurance that the decision is in safe hands, that the product will be right and the price fair. The buyer also needs to know that all promises will be kept.

Your impact on him or her, therefore, must reflect confidence, sincerity, expertise, and friendliness.

The whole subject of personal impact will be "dissected" into the sections listed above, starting with body language.

A Definition of Body Language

Body language is a means of expression conveyed by gestures, facial expressions, eye contact, and postures. It is sometimes called "non-verbal communication."

For salespeople, body language is a form of visual aid. It is used to reinforce the sales message — to help dramatize key points. And it is used to convey confidence, conviction, and other aspects that will please and assure the buyer.

Educators have known for years that we learn:
- 6 percent through taste, touch and smell
- 11 percent through hearing
- 83 percent through sight.

Professional teachers (and sales managers) make good use of these percentages. They employ blackboards, flip charts, overhead projectors, videos, and computers to help their students (and salespeople) learn by sight and sound. And, consciously or subconsciously, they use body language to strengthen their delivery.

Top-performing salespeople are like actors on a

stage: They instinctively employ body language to support their verbal presentations.

It is therefore very smart to study and use body language in your sales efforts — particularly in your handling (or preventing) of objections.

In addition, it is smart to concentrate on your prospect's body language. It can signal significant facts to help you in your presentation — thus preventing some objections and put-offs.

The Importance of Body Language In Handling Objections

The right body language can reinforce the words you use. The wrong body language can deny them. To be really effective in selling — and especially in handling objections — your verbal and visual language must complement one another.

Also, your prospect's body language can confirm or deny the words he or she uses.

It is therefore important to practice the use of the right body language to emphasize your statements — especially in your responses to objections. Likewise, it is important to study and understand the prospect's visual language and measure it against his or her words.

Body language is a combination of:
1. Facial expression and head movements
2. Gestures with hands and arms
3. Movements of the rest of the body, including the legs.

In responding to an objection, you want to present the image of a friendly, understanding, thoughtful, and confident person. In a typical sales interview, you may employ a series of combinations as you progress from the initial contact, through the dialogue, the response to the objection, and then to the close. Table 1 shows examples.

Table 1. Body Language That Creates a Positive Image

	Initial Contact	Dialogue	Response	Close
Desired Image	Confident	Friendly and Understanding	Thoughtful	Confident
Facial expression and head movement	good eye contact	smile	tilt head to one side	smile
	little eye blinking	nod head in agreement	frequent eye contact	eye contact
	chin forward	shake head in in sympathy	nod and/or shake head	head erect
Hands and arms	hands away from face	keep arms uncrossed	hand to cheek	hands away from face
	"steeple" fingertips	hands open	stroke chin, arms uncrossed	hands apart in lap or on thighs
Body	lean back, if seated	legs uncrossed	legs still	lean back
	if standing, remain erect	lean forward slightly to speak	lean forward to speak	legs out in front
	no jerking or wriggling	lean back to listen		

Body Language That Will Create Objections and Put-Offs

The opposite of "confidence" is "timidity." You create problems for yourself if you let your body language indicate unsureness and nervousness — or timidity. The prospect must be sure that his or her buying decision and business reputation is in safe hands. When your nervous mannerisms signal that you are not sure of yourself or your proposition, the prospect will use an objection or put-off to end the interview. The prospect will feel that working with you would put him or her in unsafe hands. Table 2 gives an example of body language you want to avoid:

Table 2. Body Language That Creates a Negative Image

Face and head	Swallow frequently
	Clear your throat frequently
	Lick your lips
	Avoid eye contact
	Blink your eyes frequently
Hands and arms	Open and close your hands frequently
	Tug at an ear
	Cross your arms defensively
	Fumble with your sales tools
Body	Tap your feet
	Fidget in your chair

The Prospect's Body Language

The body language of the prospect can signal either a positive or negative reaction to you or your proposition. Examples are given in Table 3.

Table 3. Understanding Your Prospect's Body Language

Prospect is	Signaling Positive Reaction	Signaling Negative Reaction
Face and head	Frequent eye contact	Blank expression
	Frequent head nods	Little eye contact
	Frequent smiling	No head nods
	Slight tilt of the head to one side	Looks down at desk
		No smile
Hands and arms	Hands and arms open Strokes chin	Arms crossed
		Fiddles with some object on desk
	Accepts literature and handles it with interest	Seems reluctant to accept or scan sales literature
Body	Uncrossed legs	Crossed legs
	Leans forward to speak	Tapping movement of foot
	Leans back to listen	Swiveling in chair

Note: If you accept buyer signals that indicate a negative, impatient attitude, you are almost certain to get an objection or a brush-off. Therefore, when that body language begins to appear, do something about it! Take action at once or you will be wasting your time in continuing the interview. Increase your test and probing questions. Use open-ended questions to force attention and response. Follow each question by silence and eye contact. Make the prospect break the silence with a reply. Get the prospect to open crossed arms by handing him or her something — such as a list of satisfied customers.

Become a student of body language. Concentrate on your prospects as you work with them. You will soon develop a "built-in radar" that will signal encouragement or warnings.

Be a "people watcher." Study their body language and match it with their words. Watch actors on stage and on TV. Watch how they reinforce their words with their gestures and posture. In most cases, 70 percent of the message is conveyed by body language.

Be a watcher of yourself. Be aware of your body language. Make it work for you in sales situations. Practice before a mirror. Follow the signals shown on the charts above. You will soon improve your "batting average" in gaining and holding favorable attention, developing a profitable dialogue, making your proposal, handling objections, and closing sales.

Vocabulary

Words are sales tools. Their precise selection for the job at hand helps you create that positive personal image that's so important to your sales efforts. Make your sales presentation concise and to the point. Do the same in responding to objections. Choose the right words to describe your proposition — and your reply to the objection. Select words to fit your prospect's comprehension. Make sure your words convey your exact meaning.

One of the best ways to select the right words of a proposition is to write your proposal in longhand. Use triple space between lines and use wide margins. Then go over your proposal again and again. Keep the specific buyer in mind. What are the most precise words to use in gaining and holding that prospect's attention? Use a dictionary to check the spelling and pronunciation of words you're unsure of. The space between lines and the wide margins will give you room for changes and improvements.

As you close in on the final draft read it aloud again and again. You will "program your brain" with those powerful words and sentences.

As you plan other calls in this manner, your vocabulary will widen. Your fluent use of the right words will make a very favorable impression — and more sales.

Incidentally, extensive research on the subject of vocabulary concluded that a broad knowledge of the exact meaning of words accompanies success. Scores on vocabulary tests are almost always in a direct ratio to the person's rank in an organization. Throughout the various levels of a given company, the managers tend to have larger vocabularies and better scores on vocabulary tests than their subordinates. It follows, then, that the development of your vocabulary will be one more asset for you as you climb the promotional ladder. And, at the same time, you will improve your personal impact.

Oral Delivery

The words you use (vocabulary) and the way you use them (delivery) are vital to your success in selling. An oral delivery can be "dissected" and examined in four major segments:
- Pronunciation
- Enunciation
- Tone
- Speed.

All four, when put together, make up what is commonly known as "delivery." Public speakers and anchor people are usually judged by the personal image they project, and part of that is derived by their delivery techniques.

Pronunciation — the act of uttering words, giving letters the correct sound and placing the accent correctly. Vocabulary-building includes practice in pronunciation with special attention to accenting.

Enunciation — the act of speaking and pronouncing words distinctly. When you form distinct sounds, syllables, and words, you are enunciating correctly.

Tone — the quality of sound. It is the general effect of the sound of your voice.

Speed — the velocity or rate of delivery. A good

speaking rate is 140-160 words per minute. A faster rate indicates nervousness and uncertainty. One of the best ways to check and improve your oral delivery is by the use of a tape recorder. Cut out a sales brochure to make a practice piece containing 160 words (double or triple it if you like). Take a deep breath and speak those words into the microphone. Time your delivery. Then play your speech back and listen for your pronunciation, enunciation, tone, and rate of delivery. Continue to practice with other pieces (including sections of your sales presentation) until you are completely satisfied with your delivery. Such planning, preparing, and practicing will go a long way toward improving and maintaining your personal impact.

Business Dress and Personal Grooming

It is obvious that proper business dress and careful personal grooming are vitally important to the development of a positive personal impact. However, both subjects can be easily overlooked during the course of a busy sales day. It is smart to put yourself in the hands of a good clothier and an expert in personal care — and follow that person's advice. Make sure that your appearance is exactly right before you "step on stage" for the serious business of selling.

It is during the day that some salespeople spoil the impression they make on others. They permit themselves to become sloppy and disheveled — and their lobby behavior is less than impressive.

Summary

This chapter covers the subject of positive personal impact and its importance in professional selling and in handling objections. We know that the salesperson who has powerful and positive personal impact encounters fewer objections than one who doesn't. That is why "personal selling" is of equal importance to "product selling."

In this chapter we examined the things that create a good impression or impact:

- Body language
- Vocabulary
- Oral delivery
- Dress
- Grooming.

When put together and used in combination, they create a synergistic effect that gains and holds favorable attention. It is suggested that you review this chapter and then answer the questions and do the exercises that follow.

Review Questions and Exercises

1. Write your description of *personal impact.*

    _____

    _____

    _____

    _____

    _____

2. List the subjects that, when combined, form
    either a positive or negative personal impact.

    _____

    _____

    _____

    _____

    _____

    _____

3. Give your definition of *body language.*

_____

_____

_____

_____

_____

_____

4. Explain the importance of body language.

_____

_____

_____

_____

_____

_____

5. Describe some of the body language signals from the prospect that denote disinterest or impatience — and describe some techniques you might use to counteract that attitude.

_____

_____

_____

_____

_____

_____

6. Why is a wide vocabulary important to the salesperson?

_____

_____

_____

_____

_____

_____

7. What are the four things that affect an oral delivery?

_____

_____

_____

_____

_____

_____

CHAPTER 4

Common Objections and Put-Offs: How to Handle Them

This chapter offers many common objections and put-offs with comments about them and suggested responses to them. It puts into specific suggestions many of the ideas advanced so far in this book. Those tips, hopefully, have started you thinking and concentrating on the objection problem. You have a better chance of success in handling objections when you follow these suggestions than you would if you just take them as they come.

Remember, however, that there are no "pat" answers in selling. Sales situations vary and people differ in their response to other people. Further, it is best when you say things in your own words (if those words are carefully chosen). You may not be comfortable with the words offered in the responses. Space is therefore provided after each objection to write your own response — using your own words. It is suggested that you add reminders to use visual aids and body language and describe the visual aids and body language you would use in detail.

In addition, discuss the responses (your own and those in this book) with your peers and your sales manager. This combined thinking can lead to the development of a treasure house of objection-handling ideas.

At the end of the next chapter, space is provided for additional common objections and those that are peculiar to your industry. Again, through discussions with others, you can add objection-handling ideas to this book for your company and your industry. The book, then, becomes a "trigger" device for the solution to many of your company's objection problems.

1. "This Won't Fit My Specifications"

Comments

This can be a legitimate objection determined by measurements or specifications. It can be an honest statement based on a misunderstanding or incorrect information. The misunderstanding can be caused by a poor presentation that is given too fast without frequent checks for comprehension. The incorrect information can be caused by incomplete product knowledge.

Recheck your product's specifications against your prospect's requirements. Also, review your presentation techniques — particularly your speed of delivery and your questioning and listening skills. Make sure you are effectively determining the needs of the prospect. The use of test questions during the interview will "nail down" prospect needs point by point and prevent misunderstanding.

Don't embarrass your prospect once you determine that your product *will* meet the specifications. Pause before you respond. Don't be cocky! Ask questions calmly and respectfully. Show by your attitude that you sincerely want to provide exactly the right product.

Suggested Response

Avoid body language that will indicate impatience — hands on hips, for example. Pause and look thoughtful.

"I'm sorry, (name of prospect). Could you

please tell me why you think this won't fit your specifications? [Listen carefully, use good eye contact — nod thoughtfully.] All right, let's review your specifications with mine — then if we can clear up that one point, we have a deal. Okay?"

Your Response

Below, write a similar response in your own words. Don't forget to insert cues for body language, testimonials, success stories and visual aids.

_____

_____

_____

_____

_____

_____

_____

2. "My Business Is Different"

Comments

This can be either a put-off or an honest statement of what the prospect really believes. You must determine if there *is* a difference and *why* such a difference should affect the sale. You are in no position to rebut the prospect's statement until you learn more about the resistance.

Your response, therefore, should be designed to continue the dialogue to determine why the business is so different that your product will not meet the need. The response should be accompanied by good eye contact, body language indicating sincere interest, and a deep respect for the prospect's opinion.

Note: Selective prospecting will reduce the number of such objections because you will know in advance of the possible needs based on your experience with customers in the same industry.

Suggested Response

"I'm sure your company is different, (prospect's name). Each company I work for is slightly different. [Pause, use good eye contact and smile.] But, in many cases, the need is the same. The need we discussed is prevalent in most companies in your industry. For example, (Customer X) felt that his company was different but we [relate success story]. [Pause and use good eye contact. Be sincere and show it.] Can you tell me how the difference in your company will affect my proposition?" [Remain silent until the prospect replies.]

Your Response

Use the space below to write one or more responses to this objection.

_____

_____

_____

_____

_____

_____

_____

_____

3. "I'm Too Busy"

Comments

This is a very common put-off used by those whose interest has not been aroused. Try to prevent the "I'm too busy" objection from arising. Before your call, prepare a list of the positive features of

your proposition and the benefits your prospect will enjoy from them. Determine in your own mind why the prospect should give you some time at the expense of other duties. Prepare a list of customers who have had problems similar to your prospect's and list the products and benefits you have provided for them. Practice using that list as a visual aid that can be quickly scanned by your prospect. (For telephone contacts, use success stories.) If these tactics don't prevent the put-off from arising, use a response similar to the one on the next page.

Suggested Response

Don't answer too quickly. Pause and look thoughtful. Use the prospect's name. Make good eye contact. Don't smile until you near the end of your response. Have your list of satisfied customers ready at the appropriate part of your response.

"Mr./Mrs. _____, I can appreciate that a person in your position is very busy. That is why I wouldn't ask you for your time if I weren't certain that you will benefit. In less than five minutes, I can show you what we have done for other companies similar to yours. [Show list.] Here is a list of some of those companies. May I tell you what we have done for them?"

Your Response

Below write one or two responses to this objection. Think of a recent sales situation in which you were given this objection or put-off.

_____

_____

_____

_____

_____

_____

4. "You'd Be Wasting Your Time"

Comments

This is a very common brush-off, especially when telephoning for an appointment. But it can also be given during a lobby interview or when you ask for permission to survey the prospect's needs.

It is possible that your prospect is sincere in the belief that you would be wasting your time. And it is also possible that your product or service isn't needed. If you get a lot of "you'd be wasting your time" objections, check your prospecting methods. Selective prospecting will reduce the number of objections of this type.

Selective prospecting means calling on prospects that are in an industry (or type of business) in which you or your company has had success in handling specific applications for your product or service. You know, then, that your selected prospect probably has that same need and, therefore, you would not be wasting your time — or the prospect's time. Further, your opening remarks can be in the vernacular of the industry — thus showing immediately that your experience could be valuable to the prospect.

Suggested Response

[Smile and shake your head.] "There are many demands on my time, (name of prospect). That's why I call (or call on) the companies that are most likely to benefit from _____ [pause and make good eye contact] as have others in your type of business.

Spending some time together, (name of prospect), could be good business. There will be no obligation on your part. When may I come to see you? Would tomorrow be okay or would the next day be more convenient?" [Remain silent until the prospect replies.]

Your Response

In the space below, write one or more of your own responses to this objection. Try them out with your peers and sales manager before you try them on your prospects.

_____

_____

_____

_____

_____

_____

_____

_____

5. "I Don't Understand"

Comments

This is a good objection because it indicates that the prospect really wants to have more information and is interested in your proposition. It is also good because it will alert you to some flaws in your sales presentation.

It is a common error to become so involved in the technical aspects of the sales presentation that we fail to think in terms of the buyer. The prospect wants to know the benefits that will be enjoyed by the use of your product or service. That is why your presentation should be made in the form of selling sentences. For example: "You will produce more units and make more profit because of the higher production speed of this machine."

Translate the features into benefits and you will encounter fewer objections of this type. Also, use test questions frequently in your sales presentation. For example, "Do you see how this will improve your production schedules and your profit goals?"

Suggested Response

"I'm sorry (prospect's name), that's my fault. [Make good eye contact and smile.] I sometimes get carried away because I'm so enthusiastic about my (product or service). Please tell me what you don't understand so we can go over it again. Okay?"

Your Response

Write your own response to this objection —
and plan the use of body language and sales tools to
reinforce what you say.

_____

_____

_____

_____

_____

_____

_____

6. "I Tried Something Like That — It Didn't Work"

Comments

This objection could be similar to "I've had a bad experience with your company" or it could be about a bad experience with a similar product from a competitor company. It is also possible that the last try was based on an incomplete or inaccurate determination of the prospect's needs — resulting in a proposal that was wrong for the problem.

The best way to handle this objection is by questioning the prospect about what happened — and why it happened. You then review your information and your proposal to make sure it won't happen again with your product.

Suggested Response

"Oh, I'm sorry, (prospect's name). [Pause and look thoughtful.] Will you please tell me what happened? [Listen intently; make notes; shake your head in sympathy; use good eye contact; make sympathetic remarks.] That put you on the spot. I'm glad you stopped it. I can see why you are reluctant to try something like that again. (Prospect's name), it's possible that the previous (product) was wrong for the job it had to perform. Let me review the information I have about your present method — and then make sure the product I recommended is right for the job. If it isn't, I'll say so. If my recommendation is right, I'd like to take you to some very successful installations where you can talk to the users. Okay?" [Followed by silence.]

Your Response

Write a response to this objection and practice using it together with supporting materials and body language.

_____

_____

_____

_____

_____

_____

_____

7. "See Me Later — No Budget for That Right Now"

Comments

This objection could be similar to "I like it, but I'm not ready for it right now." The prospect may intend to eventually buy but has no money allocated for it right now. This could be a valid delay.

On the other hand, this could be a tested put-off offered by a prospect who is indifferent to your proposal (or doesn't completely understand it) or, because of time and work pressures, doesn't want to go into it right now.

In either case, what is needed here is more dialogue. Your response must be aimed at continuing the discussion so that additional facts can be uncovered. You must learn:

1. Does the prospect really want to buy your product and, if so, when?
2. Are there points that can be clarified or added that will create interest and hold the attention of the prospect?

The tactics or techniques for continuing the dialogue are good eye contact, rewarding remarks, the paraphrase, body language indicating sincere interest, head nods, and the frequent use of the prospect's name.

Suggested Response

"All right, (prospect's name), I understand. We all have budget problems. [Smile.] Before we set a date for a call-back, would you please tell me what you like so far about my proposition?" [Pause, make good eye contact, and take notes.] What benefits are most interesting to you?

Listen carefully with your eyes and ears. Note signs of sincere enthusiasm for your product. Use probing questions to reveal a clear understanding of your proposal, such as:

"How would that help you in your operations?" Then ask:

"May I come back on (suggest a date) or would (alternative date) be better?"

Your Response

Write your response to this objection. Watch yourself in a mirror as you act out a reply to the prospect's, "See me later. I have no budget for that right now."

_____

_____

_____

_____

_____

_____

8. "I Don't Have Room for It"

Comments

This objection is similar to "This won't fit my specifications." There are two possibilities you should consider:

1. In the mind of the prospect it may be a fact that there isn't room for your product.
2. The prospect may be disinterested or misinformed. Handle the first possibility before the second one.

To work with the first possibility, position your product in the space being considered for its use. If that is impractical, have available a piece of cloth cut to the outside dimension of your product. Use it as a template as you lay it in the space being considered. (This tactic is frequently used by office equipment salespeople.) Also, of course, recheck your specifications against those of your prospect.

To handle the second possibility, review your sales presentation. Are you really attracting and holding favorable attention? One of the best ways to make sure is to ask test questions, such as, "Isn't that an interesting feature?" or "How does that look to you, (name of prospect)?"

Suggested Response

Again, handling objections is far more than saying something in reply to the prospect's negative comments. An effective response requires salesmanship, body language, and sales tools — and all of this takes thoughtful preparation and practice. For example, even though you may be certain that the prospect's comment "I don't have room for it" is incorrect, you don't show that certainty in a cocky, domineering manner. Instead, you quietly demonstrate the fact that there is room for your product. You do it so tactfully that you don't embarrass or offend your prospect.

"You may be correct, (prospect's name). Let's check it. [Take out your tape measure or cloth template mentioned above.] If it does fit, can we then review the benefits and get your favorable decision?" [Look serious at this point, maintain good eye contact — and wait for reply.]

Your Response

Write your version of the right reply to this objection below.

_____

_____

_____

_____

_____

_____

_____

_____

9. "I Like It, but I'm Not Ready for It"

Comments

This could be a valid excuse for a delay in the purchase — or it could be a put-off.

If it's a put-off, it may be that you are calling on the wrong person — one who has no authority to buy but doesn't want you to know that. On the other hand, your prospect may have the authority to buy but has other projects that may have higher priorities than yours. This *can* happen.

Review in your own mind the measurable benefits of your proposition. Are they of such importance to the prospect that it would be foolish to delay the purchase? Specifically, what will be lost by not buying now? This is where your preparatory homework pays off.

Remember, the primary objective of the response is to keep the dialogue going. In this case, your response must be designed to get a clearer picture of the prospect's authority and, if possible, to discover what some of the higher priorities might be.

In your reply, act pleased and excited when the prospect says, "I like it." Show your enthusiasm for the benefits of your product as you review them in the response. Use good eye contact and show sincere professional interest as you ask the questions as suggested in the response.

Suggested Response

"Thank you, that's good, (prospect's name). [Smile.] I'm so glad you like my proposition. [Show list of benefits.] As we discussed, it will provide these benefits: _____,
_____, _____. You can start to enjoy those benefits immediately."
If your prospect remains indecisive, ask the following questions:
"Could you tell me what must take precedence over those advantages?"
"Are there others involved in making the decision on my proposition?"

Your Response

Think of a prospect who gave you this objection. Imagine yourself facing that buyer now — and write your response that will fit that sales situation. Synchronize your words with body language and the use of visual aids and other sales tools. Practice your response with your colleagues.

_____

_____

_____

_____

_____

_____

10. "I've Had a Bad Experience with Your Company"

Comments

Perhaps your prospect *did* have some bad experiences with your company. It's possible. Many companies have their "ups and downs" in terms of good quality and customer satisfaction. Whether the bad feeling is fair or unfair, it *is* in the mind of the buyer. You can't proceed to the sale until you clear up this real or imagined "bad experience."

Draw out the prospect by polite questioning and good listening. Good listening means listening with your eyes *and* ears. Study the prospect's body language and the tone of voice, as well as the words and delivery. Keep the dialogue going by using rewarding remarks such as:

"I understand."

"Nice going!"

"That was good thinking, (prospect's name)."

Also, use the paraphrase such as:

"(Prospect's name), a minute ago you said (repeat those comments)."

Show by your body language that you're interested, sincere in your desire to correct the situation, and sympathetic to the prospect's position. You do this by head nod, head shake, frown, open stance [arms unfolded], and good eye contact. Be just as emphatic as the prospect in your belief that companies should deliver quality products at the right price and with the promised delivery schedule. You can do this without actually criticizing your company.

Suggested Response

"I'm sorry you feel that way, (prospect's name). [Look surprised, pause, stand motionless, use good eye contact.] Will you please tell me what happened? [Look very sincere, maintain good eye contact and show you are listening intently by taking notes.] Well, (prospect's name), I'm sorry that happened and I'll report this to my manager. I've heard of some problems in the past, but that was some time ago. [Use prospect's name to indicate a change in pace.] I can give you the names of many satisfied customers that I personally service. Here are some thank you letters from a few of them. [Always have some strong testimonial letters in your briefcase ready for quick showing without fumbling. This takes practice.] I promise to check this out. Now, may I show you a superb line of (product name) backed up by a 100 percent guarantee and my promise of personal attention to your orders?"

Your Response

Use this space to write your own response to this objection. To successfully handle this one, well planned body language, testimonials, and success stories are essential.

_____

_____

_____

_____

_____

_____

_____

_____

11. "I Can't Afford It"

Comments

This objection is similar to "I like it, but I'm not ready for it right now" and "See me later — no budget for that right now."

Without the proper research and qualification, it is possible to propose something to the prospect that is out of the money range or is unrealistic in terms of needs. To prevent the "I can't afford it" objection near the end of your presentation, use probing questions during the interview. You must get a clear picture of the prospect's present course of action and the goals for improvement. If those questions reveal that your proposal *is* impractical, you are honor bound to say so before the prospect

does. If, on the other hand, your questions uncover certain possible improvements that you can offer, you then have an ethical course to pursue.

Ask probing questions such as:

1. How many units per day do you produce?
2. How many units per day would you like to produce?
3. What is your production cost per unit?

Answers to such questions will give you an idea of the possible improvement your product can provide that will make its purchase practical.

Here, again, is the need for the consultative approach. The right questions — and your professional conduct and attitude — will help keep the dialogue going. And that dialogue will soon reveal 1) if your proposal is unrealistic or 2) whether the benefits from the use of your product will make the purchase a savings rather than an unnecessary expense.

Suggested Response

[Smile, nod head in agreement and pause.] "You may be right, [use prospect's name frequently]. I can understand why you can't afford it if it's an unnecessary expense. Here's a letter from a very happy customer. [Show testimonial letter.] This company [give the name of the customer] also felt it couldn't afford it, but that gave me the opportunity to go into my proposition in more detail and here is what we found (success story). We discovered that my product was not an expense. Instead, the purchase became a savings. We may be able to do the same for you. May I have your permission to do some research on your present plan?" [Remain silent until the prospect replies.]

Your Response

Picture an actual sales situation in which your prospect said, "I can't afford it." Now, using the ideas in this book, write a reply that will fit that interview.

_____

_____

_____

_____

_____

_____

_____

_____

12. "Let Me Talk It Over with ——"

Comments

There can be many valid reasons for "Let me talk it over with _____." Many large companies require multiple decisions for a single purchase. A purchasing agent, for example, would not buy factory equipment without first talking it over with the factory manager. It's more than just talking it over. The factory manager must approve the purchase after making sure the product will fit the needs.

This objection can be prevented by recognizing in advance the possibility of a multiple decision situation. The size of the prospect organization and the type of product can determine this. If possible, call first on the decision maker (such as the factory manager). In many cases this can't be done without offending the one who finally issues the purchase order. If such is the case, your mission, when you call on the purchasing person, is to get him or her enthusiastic enough to permit you to see the decision maker.

Good salesmanship is needed in this situation. You must be prepared for this objection. Have ready (or list during the interview) the benefits of your proposal. Don't depend on the official company sales brochure. Attach a written list that can be quickly and easily read — and understood. Make sure the purchasing agent understands the benefits and is sold and enthusiastic about your proposal.

Suggested Response Number 1

"I can appreciate that others should be con-
sulted (prospect's name), before you make your
decision. [Smile and pause.] To save your time,
would you please call those other executives,
and I'll see each one to explain the benefits of
my proposition. Then I'll call you for another
appointment. Okay?" [Remain silent until your
prospect replies.]

Suggested Response Number 2

When suggested response number 1 fails, or is
impractical to try, say:
"Okay, (prospect's name), could we review this
list of features and benefits? Then I'll leave it
with you to show the other executives." [Show
enthusiasm and review the benefits.] Now,
(prospect's name), when may I return for your
decision?" [As you ask that question, take out
your appointment book and be prepared to
write; remain silent until your prospect replies.]

Your Response

In the space below write your response to this objection.

_____

_____

_____

_____

_____

_____

_____

_____

13. "Drop Something in the Mail" or "Leave Your Catalog"

Comments

This is another common put-off. It could be caused by disinterest in you and/or your proposition — or it could be caused by severe time or work pressures.

"Drop something in the mail" is usually offered during a telephone conversation. Another version is "Leave your catalog," suggested during a face-to-face interview. In either case, when this happens to you, chances are you have not captured favorable attention. The buyer isn't telling you that in blunt terms. You are being politely brushed-off so the prospect can get rid of you and on to something else that takes a higher priority.

Review your sales presentation. It's not working for you. The best way to handle this objection is to prevent it from happening. Think in terms of the prospect. Review your customer records. What customers do you have that are in a line of business similar to that of your prospect? What benefits were you able to provide those customers that might also apply to your prospect? Develop a selling sentence that will clearly communicate those benefits to your prospect. Here's an example:

"(Name of prospect), my company has provided these benefits to many companies in your industry. For example, we have done _____ for (company name). It is possible that we could offer you the same benefits. When may I come to your office to discuss this possibility with you?"

Before making the call, prepare visual aids that are easily read and understood, such as graphs and "bottom line" figures. Also, be prepared with testimonial letters as well as success stories from satisfied customers. Make your presentation in terms of possible benefits to the prospect and the prospect's company.

Suggested Response

"Frankly, Mr./Mrs. _____, sending a brochure is not the answer. I know what we have done for other companies similar to yours, but that information is worthless unless it relates to your particular situation. It won't take me long to determine what benefits we can offer you. When may I discuss this with you?" [Remain silent until the prospect answers.]

Your Response

Try one or two responses of your own. Picturing a real-life sales situation in which this objection was given by your prospect will help you select the right words.

_____

_____

_____

_____

_____

CHAPTER 5

More Common Objections And How to Handle Them

14. "I'll Wait Until Business Gets Better"

Comments

In the mind of the buyer there are nine questions to be answered. They are in the buyer's mind either consciously or subconsciously. The questions are:

1. Why should I see you?
2. Why should I listen?
3. What's my problem?
4. How is it solved?
5. Why should I trust you?
6. Why should I trust your company?
7. Why is your solution best?
8. Why should I take action?
9. Why should I take action *now*?

When your prospect says, "I'll wait until business gets better," you are faced with either an honest objection (as the prospect sees it) or a stall. If it's a stall, you have failed in the answers to questions 1 through 8 above. If it's an honest worry about current economic conditions, you are faced only with answering question 9.

The stall can sometimes be prevented by asking test questions as you proceed through your sales presentation. They can be employed as you proceed down the list of the first eight questions above. For example, for question 3 you can ask, "Are we agreed on the problem?" Likewise, for question 4 ask, "Are we agreed that my proposal will solve this problem?" If you have not "buttoned down" your presentation point by point (thus causing the stall), review those points in your response.

Suggested Response Number 1

"(Prospect's name), business is down for some people right now. [Pause and look concerned.] But I didn't realize your business was suffering. [Look around admiringly.] I'm sure it's just a temporary lull. [Pause.] I'm glad you like my proposal and will buy when you can. Specifically, what do you like most about it? How do you think it will help you? If business conditions were right, would you buy right now?" [Use good body language as you ask these questions, show sincere and professional interest, listen with your eyes and ears, watch for a sincere and enthusiastic response by the prospect. If the prospect assures you that it's not a stall, then proceed to suggested response number 2.]

Suggested Response Number 2

"(Prospect's name), we have reviewed the benefits you can start enjoying the minute your new (product) is installed. By waiting until this temporary lull is over, these are the losses you

will suffer _____. Further, during
the lull we will have more time to concentrate
on the installation of (product), and we can
keep your employees busy while they learn
about the more efficient uses of the _____.
We can arrange convenient terms for you and,
in the meantime, you will have the use of
_____. Okay?"

Your Response

As you write some of your own responses to
this objection or put-off, don't forget to plan your
body language and supporting sales tools.

_____

_____

_____

_____

_____

_____

_____

_____

15. "Your Price Is Too High"

Comments

This common objection has probably been one of the major reasons for lost sales in every salesperson's career. It is used by many buyers either 1) as a put-off or 2) as a maneuver for the opening of negotiations for a lower price. If it's a put-off, the prospect doesn't see or understand the benefits you offer and wants to close the interview. If it is a maneuver for a lower price, your prospect wants to buy, and you are on the road to a sale — provided your response is planned and effective.

If you are getting a lot of "Your price is too high" objections, first review your sales presentation. Are you gaining and holding favorable attention? Are you developing an effective, informative dialogue to determine the needs and the "hot buttons" of the prospect? Are you making your proposal in terms of specific, measurable benefits? Are you using test questions to check for understanding and agreements?

Remember, *price must always be weighed against value.* You cannot consider price without also considering the value to be received for that price. So, when your prospect says, "Your price is too high," ask yourself, "Compared to what?" In other words, make sure you and your prospect are talking about the same values.

Values include more than just the features of the product. In addition to the benefits derived from specific mechanical features, you must also include service coverage and facilities, parts and supply availability, storage proximity, guarantee, shipping

costs and facilities, and the expertise of your backup
team at the branch or home office. These additional
values can weigh in your favor when the product
itself is only equal to, but not better, than a competitive product.

There is another important value, too. That
value is you. It is your personality, your reputation,
your record for caring and service, and your tactful
handling of details that are all weighed in the buying
decision. When you "sell yourself" as well as sell
your product, price becomes relatively unimportant.
In fact, a recent study shows that only 6 percent of all
buyers base their decision strictly on price alone.
Buying is done with the heart as well as with the
head.

Your response, therefore, should be planned to accomplish two things:

1. To keep the dialogue going, so you can determine the basis for the prospect's objection and the values he or she is considering.
2. To continue to sell yourself as an ethical professional with whom your prospect can feel secure in his or her buying decision.

Suggested Response Number 1

"(Prospect's name), as you know so well, we can't talk about price without considering the value that price provides. I'm sure you will agree to that. [Pause and look for some sign of interest and agreement.] So, let's review the benefits my price will give you. [Review the benefits to be gained.] Also, (prospect's name), the initial cost of my _____ is about the same as my competitor's, but my proposal offers these additional values: _____, _____, _____, _____. [Pause, look very serious, maintain good eye contact.] In addition, (prospect's name), I know my product has an estimated life of _____. I'd be happy to take you to some satisfied customers who will confirm that estimate. Over the lifetime of my product, you will be enjoying these savings _____ and these benefits _____. When may I deliver this to you?"

Suggested Response Number 2

This response is suggested when your product is superior and also higher priced than your competitor's. Your product has certain features that are better than the competitor's. In this case, *bring up the subject of price before your prospect does.*

"(Prospect's name), my _____ is probably about _____ percent higher than my competitor's — and here's why. [Use selling sentences that explain the additional benefits gained because of the superior features.] When you consider the many years of additional benefits, I think you will agree that the initial price is relatively unimportant. Don't you agree?"

Your Response

Think of some sales situations in which you have encountered the price objection. Keep those interviews in mind as you write some responses to them.

_____

_____

_____

_____

_____

_____

16. "I'll Think About It"

Comments

This common objection has ruined many potential sales. At first glance, it seems to be an innocent delay and a reasonable request for more decision time. It isn't. There are many possible reasons advanced for "I'll think about it," but they all boil down to a common few:

1. Your prospect hasn't the authority to buy and doesn't want to tell you that the decision-making authority is in the hands of another.
2. The buyer has doubts about you, your company, or your product.

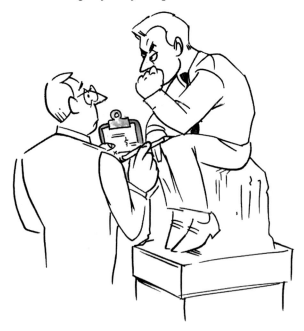

3. Time and work pressures put your proposal low on the prospect's priority list.
4. Your prospect doesn't understand all the details of your proposition and doesn't want to ask for more information.
5. The buyer just isn't interested and doesn't want to be discourteous.

Buyers have found that the "I'll think about it" objection is an effective put-off. They can satisfy the need for being courteous to visiting salespeople, give them as little time as possible, and then dismiss them politely — thus freeing themselves for (in their judgment) more important things.

Your sales presentation must be planned to prevent this objection from arising. Load it with probing questions to handle problems number 1 and 2 above. State the benefits clearly and concisely and then use test questions to handle problems number 3, 4, and 5 above.

Plan your response to recheck all of the problems listed above, uncover the real reason for the objection, and keep the dialogue going until it's time to proceed to the close.

Suggested Response

"That's a wise decision, (prospect's name), to think it over. [Pause, smile, show enthusiasm, and maintain good eye contact.] Let's think it over together. First, let's talk about the primary benefit. [Use a selling sentence to describe the benefit provided by the positive feature, then ask a test question to assure understanding and interest.] Are we agreed that this will be an important benefit, (prospect's name)? [Remain silent and wait for the reply.] What are some of the other things you like about my proposal? [The reply will give you a clear picture of the prospect's interest and understanding.] Are there others involved in making the decision on this — or is it entirely up to you to decide? [These questions and replies will cover the five points listed in the comments and clear the way for asking for the order. Assuming the prospect says that he or she is the only decision maker, ask a closing question.] Okay, then. When would you like this delivered?"

Your Response

Write your own responses to this objection and discuss them with your peers and sales manager.

_____

_____

_____

_____

_____

_____

_____

_____

17. "I'm Satisfied with My Present Suppliers"

Comments

Your prospect may be telling you the truth. Competitive suppliers may be offering excellent service to the account. But the buyer may also be fearful of change and the possible criticism from his or her boss or colleagues. People are inclined to "leave well enough alone."

Buyers are also loyal to sellers who give them good service and make them feel safe in their buying decisions. The loyalty your prospect has for your competitors is the very same loyalty you must win and maintain.

It is therefore very important that you do not criticize your competitors. This can be construed as criticism of your prospect's buying decisions. You can, however, get the prospect to do the criticizing for you when you ask the questions shown in the response.

Keep this in mind: A change will not be made making you the supplier until you prove that the change is safe for the buyer as a person as well as safe for the buying company. Therefore, a trusting relationship is vital to your success in this situation. Display a thoughtful, sincere attitude. Be prepared with proofs of customer satisfaction in the form of testimonials and success stories. Practice handling the testimonials and telling the success stories until they become smooth parts of your sales presentation. Employ good eye contact, head nods, smiles, and rewarding remarks.

Suggested Response

"I can appreciate that, (prospect's name). I'm sure you have made some very shrewd selections of your present suppliers. The buyers over at the (customer company) felt the same way about their suppliers until I showed them what we had done for other companies. They gave me a trial order and here's what happened. [Tell success story]. (Prospect's name), what are your most critical requirements in the supply of (product)? [This question gets the prospect thinking about his or her critical needs, objectives and standards of quality, delivery and service.] (Prospect's name), based on what you have just described as your most critical concerns, are those standards being met exactly as you expect them?" [This second question gets the prospect thinking about possible problems with present suppliers and perhaps some problems with quality or delivery. This review of past events may cause the prospect to analyze the present course of action and stimulate interest in trying a new supplier. Also, such questions make you appear to the prospect as a consultative professional with whom a trusting relationship can be developed.]

Your Response

Since this is a very common objection you must have experienced many like it. From the ideas offered in this book, write a response to this objection.

_____

_____

_____

_____

_____

_____

_____

_____

18. "I'm Not Interested"

Comments

This could be a legitimate objection. It is possible that the prospect doesn't really need what you are selling.

Instead of the prospect saying, "I don't need it," he or she says, "I'm not interested." Check your customer lists. If you have sold other companies in the same business category as your prospect, there is a good chance that the prospect may have a similar need for your product. If, however, your company records show no installations in that business category, the chances are that the prospect is correct. There is no interest because there is no need.

On the other hand, this may be a put-off similar to "I'm too busy," "Drop something in the mail," or "I'll think about it." These brush-offs can be caused by: 1) lack of understanding, 2) a poor sales presentation, or 3) time and work pressures. If your sales presentation was not complete, and the prospect doesn't understand your proposition, the "I'm not interested" objection will be offered to save time.

If you get a lot of "I'm not interested" objections:

1. Select your prospects from categories where the needs are known.
2. Review your sales presentation, especially in the attention-getting stage. Also, make sure your proposition is clearly stated with few possibilities of misunderstanding — or failure to understand.
3. Add test questions to your presentation to make sure your prospect is with you point by point.

Suggested Response

There are two responses shown below: 1) handling this objection when calling on the telephone for an appointment, and 2) when face to face with your prospect. Both should be practiced so that your voice and manner indicate confidence and tactful insistence.

Suggested Response Number 1

"I understand how you feel, (prospect's name). Mr./Mrs./Ms. _____ of the _____ Company, felt the same way until he/she had the opportunity to see the many things our product could do for him/her. That's why I called you for an appointment. We may be able to do the same for you. Will tomorrow be convenient for you — or will the next day suit you better?"

Suggested Response Number 2

[Use good eye contact, smile, and nod your head, have a testimonial letter from a satisfied customer in your hand and ready to show, pause before you respond, and act confident but not cocky.] "I understand, (prospect's name). You can't be interested with just a few details. (Name of satisfied customer), of the _____ Company, felt the same way, but gave me some time to go into it in detail. Here is what (name of satisfied customer) said in this complimentary letter. [Show testimonial letter.] Now, (prospect's name), I know your

time is valuable. Would it be convenient if I
came back tomorrow — or would the next day
be better for you?"

Your Response

This is a very common objection. Think of a
similar objection you encountered in a recent sales
interview. Picture that prospect and that sales
situation as you write a response to "I'm not interested."

_____

_____

_____

_____

_____

_____

_____

_____

19. "I Don't Trust You"

Comments

This objection, "I don't trust you," is usually unspoken, but is frequently the most dominant reason for not buying — or for not granting an interview — or for employing one of the common put-offs.

Buyers are just like other people. They are inclined to make snap judgments and to take instant measurements of others. Buyers must feel comfortable and safe in their buying decisions. Their business reputations are made and maintained by smart buys — just as yours is made and maintained by smart selling practices.

Therefore, your approach, your sales presentation, and your actions after the sale should be designed to develop a trusting relationship — as well as to sell your product or service. A trusting relationship can sometimes override other objections and will definitely influence the sale. When that secure feeling exists about you, the sale has come a long way toward completion — providing, of course, the need is there, and your product or service will fill that need.

How do you build a trusting relationship? The most difficult stage is in the initial contact when you appear as a complete stranger to the prospect. The less difficult stage is after the sale is made and you can demonstrate your integrity by good service and sincere followthrough.

Before and during the initial contact: Before you contact the prospect, find out as much as you can about the prospect and the company. For example, check your customer records for companies that might have the same needs as your prospect's company. What has your product or service done to satisfy the needs of those customers? What are the measurable benefits for them that you can now describe to your prospect? That knowledge will help generate that air of know-how and confidence that is so important in that initial contact. Proper dress and good grooming are vital to achieve that "ensemble of professionalism."

Be on time and be polite and gracious to everyone you encounter on the prospect's premises. Plan on showing testimonial letters and telling success stories. During the interview, be honest in your statements and sincere in your desire to discover the prospect's needs.

Use good eye contact, a thoughtful demeanor, pause before replying, stroke your chin in deep thought, use appropriate head nods and head shakes, and take notes.

In summary, demonstrate by your words and body language your sincere interest in the prospect and the company's needs — and your complete confidence that you can improve the present course of action.

After the initial contact and after the sale is made: Continue to demonstrate your reliability and dependability by keeping your word, follow up to assure complete satisfaction, and, in general, maintain a sincere seller-buyer, friend-friend relationship. It will pay off in profitable repeat business.

Suggested Response

There is no single, verbal response to this objection. Actions are more powerful than words to overcome the unspoken mistrust of the prospect. The handling of this objection must be included in the handling of all other objections.

Your Response

Since there isn't a verbal response to this unspoken resistance, reread the comments about this objection and then describe how you would handle it when you sense distrust.

_____

_____

_____

_____

_____

20. "I Have a Friend in Your Business"

Comments

This could be a put-off that the prospect has successfully used many times when there is no interest in the proposal — or the buyer is unimpressed with the salesperson. If you suspect a brush-off, double-check your presentation and your personal impact.

An honest statement by the prospect that he or she is buying from a friend or relative is a tough one to handle when the product or service is basically the same.

First, do not criticize your competitor or the competitor's product. When you do that, you also criticize the prospect's buying judgment.

Second, make an objective determination of the benefits to be gained by switching to your product. The benefits of the change must outweigh the feelings of loyalty to the friend.

Use selling sentences that describe the benefits to be derived from the positive features of your product. Be sure to include additional values such as: speed of delivery, shipping charges, warranty, corporate image, testimonials of satisfied customers, and service back-up facilities. As you do that, you tactfully force the prospect to compare what you are offering to what is being supplied by the friend or relative. You subtly encourage the prospect to review his or her previous buying decisions.

Suggested Response

[Smile, nod your head, and maintain good eye contact.] "I can understand why you wish to buy from your friend and I admire your loyalty. That is the way to go when everything is equal. But I'm sure your good friend would want you to purchase what is best for you. Let's go over the features of my product (or service) and the benefits you will enjoy from its use. Okay?"

Your Response

Write your own response in the space below.

_____

_____

_____

_____

_____

_____

_____

_____

21. "No Thanks — Just Looking"

Comments

In many cases this is not an objection. It is a response by an idle stroller in a store who has no particular purpose in mind. But also, in many cases, it's given by a prospective customer who has a definite objective and wants to do some preliminary looking before asking for the help of a salesperson.

For the effective handling of this reply, the salesperson must be very observant. A lot depends on the actions of the customer as he or she walks down the aisles. If there are only casual glances at the items on display, the chances are those articles are of little interest to the stroller.

If, however, the shopper stops and looks intently at a certain dress, for example, she might be a very good prospect. In such a case, the approach by the salesperson should be quite different from the traditional: "May I help you?" which is likely to bring the objection: "No thanks, I'm just looking."

Instead the salesperson should approach the customer, smile, nod at the dress on display, and say, "You have very good taste — that dress is really lovely and would be perfect for you. Would you like to try it on?"

If the customer's reply is, "No thanks — I'm just looking," there is a response that will keep the dialogue going and maintain the possibility of a sale without putting too much pressure on the customer.

Suggested Response

[Smile, nod your head and maintain good eye contact. Start to turn away from the customer and then turn back.] Say, "I suggest that you check out the next rack also. There are some beautiful dresses there that have just arrived. Perhaps you will find just what you are looking for. I'll be here to help if you need me."

Your Response

You have probably used this same objection when shopping. What reply from the salesperson would make you react favorably? Write that response.

_____

_____

_____

_____

_____

_____

_____

22. "I Like the Print but Not the Color"

Comments

This objection can be raised because of misunderstanding or lack of information. For example, the customer likes the print but not the color, and it becomes an objection simply because of incomplete information — that the print comes in a variety of colors. This type of objection is relatively easy to handle because it simply requires that you clarify the facts. And, of course, as in all objections, you must know your product line so that the availability of additional colors is your "reserve ammunition." Rephrase the objection in the form of a probing question.

Suggested Response

[Nod your head, look thoughtful, and maintain good eye contact.] Say, "I see. You said before that the size and design are right, and you like the print but not the color. Is the color the only reason you're reluctant to go ahead with this couch right now?" [Remain silent until the customer replies.]

Note: This tactic will help isolate the problem and perhaps get a definite commitment — providing, of course, you can supply the right color.

Your Response

Think of a similar objection you get from prospects about an item in your product line. Write a response that will: 1) help you determine if it's an honest objection or a put-off, 2) get a commitment on other features of the product, 3) get an advance commitment on the feature in question so that, if that is satisfied, you have a sale.

_____

_____

_____

_____

_____

_____

_____

23. "I Don't Like Your Delivery Schedule"

Comments

This objection can be easy or difficult to handle depending on your company's willingness to be flexible with its delivery schedule.

Also, it is possible in some cases to get the prospect to change the delivery demands. In other words, the delivery requirements might be over-stated.

The key tactic here is to keep the dialogue going so that the real facts can be discovered. Use a probing question.

Suggested Response

"I see. When do you want it?"

Note: Asking that question is another way to ask for the order. When the prospect gives you the desired receiving date, you are also being told that you have the order or at least the decision is favorable, providing you can negotiate an acceptable delivery date.

There is no "pat" answer to the solution to the delivery problem. One of the keys, however, is your attitude and behavior when discussing it. When you show sincere concern for the customer's satisfaction, you have taken a giant step toward getting the customer to "bend a little" in his or her delivery demands. Likewise, that same air of caring could influence your company to make special arrangements for the delivery.

Your Response

Write your own response to the "I don't like your delivery schedule," objection How will you use your response to close the sale?

_____

_____

_____

_____

_____

24. "I Just Don't Feel Good About This (Product, Color, Size, etc.)"

Comments

This is a good objection because it reveals careful consideration of the possible purchase and that the prospect has a definite purpose in mind. This also gives you another opportunity to show that you are a consultative salesperson.

Suggested Response

[Pause and look thoughtful.] "If you don't feel good about it, it isn't right for you. Your satisfaction is the most important consideration. Let's try to pinpoint the problem so that I'll be able to show you something you'll feel *is* right for you."

Your Response

Write your own response to this objection. If you have received a similar objection, visualize the prospect and the sales situation as you select the right words and actions to handle it.

_____

_____

_____

_____

_____

_____

_____

_____

25. "I Don't Need Service That Often"

Comments

This type of objection can arise in the sale of service contracts. It is frequently offered after the sale of a car when the dealer sets up a periodic service schedule for the car owner suggesting that certain inspection checks should be made by the dealer service department.

Unfortunately, attempts to sell such service agreements often do not include a listing of the benefits to be enjoyed by preventive maintenance.

The sale of service requires the same high degree of salesmanship as does the sale of the product. Selling sentences (described elsewhere in this book) should be practiced and used when selling services.

Suggested Response

"I understand how you feel, (prospect's name). But I am not suggesting service. I am recommending a plan of preventive maintenance. [Pause and repeat the prospect's name.] You own a very valuable piece of equipment. It is now in perfect condition. Let's keep it that way. We will greatly reduce the possibility of expensive breakdowns by the regular inspection of your _____. Many of my customers have extended the normal life of their equipment by regularly scheduled inspections. I can give you the names of customers who have used my service for many years. [Use testimonials and

success stories.] I suggest that you use the plan
for at least the first period and then review the
advantages again with me. Okay?"

Your Response

You have probably used this objection in
dealing with car and/or appliance service people.
Write a response that would appeal to you and
encourage you to buy the proposition offered.

_____

_____

_____

_____

_____

_____

_____

On the following pages, space is provided for
additional objections peculiar to your industry —
and your responses to them. By listing objections you
frequently come across, and working out responses
to them, you will be able to customize this book for
your specific use. This will make this book an even
more valuable sales tool.

Additional Objection

_____

_____

_____

_____

_____

_____

_____

_____

Your Response

_____

_____

_____

_____

_____

_____

_____

_____

Additional Objection

_____

_____

_____

_____

_____

_____

_____

_____

Your Response

_____

_____

_____

_____

_____

_____

_____

_____

Additional Objection

_____

_____

_____

_____

_____

_____

_____

Your Response

_____

_____

_____

_____

_____

_____

_____

_____

Additional Objection

_____

_____

_____

_____

_____

_____

_____

_____

Your Response

_____

_____

_____

_____

_____

_____

_____

_____

Additional Objection

_____

_____

_____

_____

_____

_____

_____

_____

Your Response

_____

_____

_____

_____

_____

_____

_____

_____

Additional Objection

_____

_____

_____

_____

_____

_____

_____

_____

Your Response

_____

_____

_____

_____

_____

_____

_____

_____

Additional Objection

_____

_____

_____

_____

_____

_____

_____

Your Response

_____

_____

_____

_____

_____

_____

_____

_____

Additional Objection

_____

_____

_____

_____

_____

_____

_____

Your Response

_____

_____

_____

_____

_____

_____

_____

_____

Additional Objection

_____

_____

_____

_____

_____

_____

_____

_____

Your Response

_____

_____

_____

_____

_____

_____

_____

_____